JULIUS CAESAR

Written by
Anita Ganeri

Illustrated by
Laura Sua

CONTENTS

Collins

ROME

At the beginning of the 1st century BCE, Rome was
the most powerful city in the world. It ruled the lands
around the Mediterranean Sea, from modern-day France
to North Africa, and beyond.

the Roman Empire in
the 1st century BCE

Britain

Atlantic
Ocean

Germany

France

Spain

Italy

ROME

Mediterranean Sea

Greece

North Africa

Lands ruled by Rome

Rome was **governed** by a group of men, called senators.
They usually came from rich and important Roman families.
Together, they were called the Senate. They met in the Senate
House in Rome to talk about the army, law and order, and how
Rome should be run.

The two most important officials were called consuls. They were
in charge of the Senate and the Roman army.

EARLY DAYS

Gaius Julius Caesar was born in July 100 BCE into a rich and important Roman family. His father, who had the same name, was a senator. The family lived in a large house in a crowded neighbourhood, called the Subura.

Julius didn't go to school. He was taught at home by a tutor, called Marcus Antonius Gnipho. Marcus quickly saw that Julius was very good at writing and learning different languages.

FACT

Like many Romans, Julius was given three names. He was called Gaius as that was his father's name. Julius came from Julii, the name of the group to which his family belonged. Caesar was the surname of his close family.

a statue of Julius Caesar as a young man

GROWING UP

Like all Roman boys, Julius officially became an adult when he was about 14 years old. A special ceremony was held where Julius was given an adult's **toga** to wear. This is a long piece of cloth that's wrapped around the body and worn over a short **tunic**.

Julius also stopped wearing his bulla, which was a **charm** worn around the neck. All children wore a bulla to keep away evil spirits.

When he was 16 years old, Julius's father died suddenly and Julius became head of the family. He had to look after his mother and sister. He also got married to Cornelia, the daughter of one of the most important men in Rome. This marriage helped Julius to start his career in politics, but the couple were also happy together and had a baby daughter, called Julia.

bulla

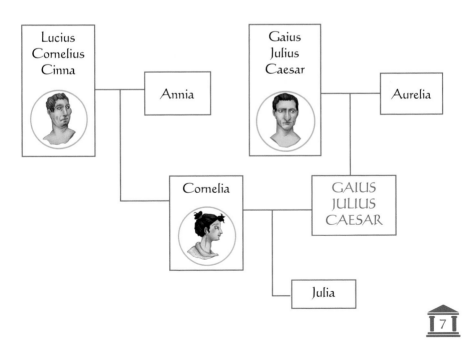

Lucius Cornelius Cinna

Annia

Gaius Julius Caesar

Aurelia

Cornelia

GAIUS JULIUS CAESAR

Julia

DANGER IN ROME

At that time, Rome was a dangerous place to live.
There were two groups of people who wanted to have all
the power in Rome. One was called the Populares and
the other was called the Optimates. There was lots of
fighting between the two groups.

Caesar's family was on the side of the Populares. His uncle
had led the group before his death. Afterwards, Caesar's
father-in-law, Cinna, became leader.

When Cinna was killed in the fighting, the Populares knew they'd lost. The Senate chose the leader of the Optimates, a man called Sulla, to be **dictator**. This meant that Sulla now had control of all officials and the Roman army.

Sulla didn't like Caesar because Caesar's family supported the Populares, and Caesar's wife, Cornelia, was Cinna's daughter. Sulla told Caesar to divorce Cornelia to show his loyalty to Rome. Caesar refused, but he'd made a dangerous enemy. The safest thing now was for him to leave Rome.

FLEEING ROME

Caesar went to Turkey, which was ruled by Rome, and joined the Roman army. He was only 19 years old, but Caesar quickly showed that he was a brilliant soldier. The Roman **governor** of Turkey sent Caesar on an important mission to stop the people on the nearby island of Lesbos fighting against them. Caesar fought bravely and helped to stop the rebellion.

While Caesar was on another mission in Turkey, he was captured by pirates. Pirates often took people prisoner because they could make money by demanding a large **ransom** from a prisoner's family or friends. Caesar's friends in Rome *did* send money and he was freed. Unluckily for the pirates, Caesar then came back in a warship and took them prisoner. He then executed them.

BACK TO ROME

After he'd been in Turkey for four years, Caesar found out that Sulla had died. It was now safe for him to return to Rome. Back home, he began working in the law courts and he became a popular lawyer. Caesar wanted to help poor people and make their lives better.

When Caesar's wife, Cornelia, died, he married Pompeia, Sulla's granddaughter. But the marriage only lasted a few years.

As well as being a lawyer, Caesar was put in charge of putting on gladiator fights and wild beast shows. These shows were held in a big **arena**, and men would fight each other with weapons.

Romans would also come to the arena to see animals like lions and tigers. Caesar worked hard to impress the people of Rome, and the games were a great success.

Three years later, Caesar was made governor of Spain. He was also given the special title of imperator (commander), after successfully fighting against Rome's enemies in Spain. This was one of the greatest honours in Rome.

Back in Rome, Caesar made a **pact** with Pompey and Crassus, two of the richest and most important men in the city. They helped him to become consul, one of the top jobs in Rome. Caesar also got married again, to a senator's daughter, called Calpurnia.

CAESAR GOES TO GAUL

The following year, 58 BCE, Caesar became governor of Gaul.
At that time, "Gaul" was the name given to an area that today
we call France. Over the next eight years, Caesar and his army
brought the whole of Gaul under Roman rule. Caesar was
a brilliant general, using clever **tactics** to beat his enemies.
Sometimes, he did this without fighting. He talked to some
of the Gaulish chiefs and persuaded them to come over
to the Romans' side.

But not everyone wanted to be under Roman rule. One chief, Vercingetorix, led the Gauls against the Romans. He won several battles, but Caesar finally defeated him and took him prisoner. Caesar liked Vercingetorix's courage, but he later took him back to Rome and had him put to death.

FACT

Julius wrote about what he had seen and done in Gaul in a book called *Commentaries on the Gallic Wars*. It was written in **Latin** and is still one of the most important history books.

Vercingetorix was held prisoner for five years before being put to death.

INVADING BRITAIN

Three years later, Caesar sailed with 80 ships and around 12,000 men across the English Channel to Britain. The Romans knew nothing about Britain, except that it was rich in lead, gold and tin. But there hadn't been enough time to plan the attack properly. The Britons fought bravely and held back the Romans. Caesar went back to Gaul, defeated.

A year later, in 54 BCE, Caesar tried again with a bigger army of 30,000 men and even an elephant. This time, he was better prepared. He was able to beat the Britons back and also held talks with some of the chiefs. But the weather was terrible and some of the Roman ships were wrecked. Once again, Caesar went back to Rome without **conquering** Britain. He never returned.

FACT

Almost 100 years later, in 43 CE, Emperor Claudius sent another army to invade Britain. This time, the Romans conquered southern Britain and made it part of the Roman Empire. The Romans finally left Britain in 410 CE.

17

CAESAR MARCHES INTO ROME

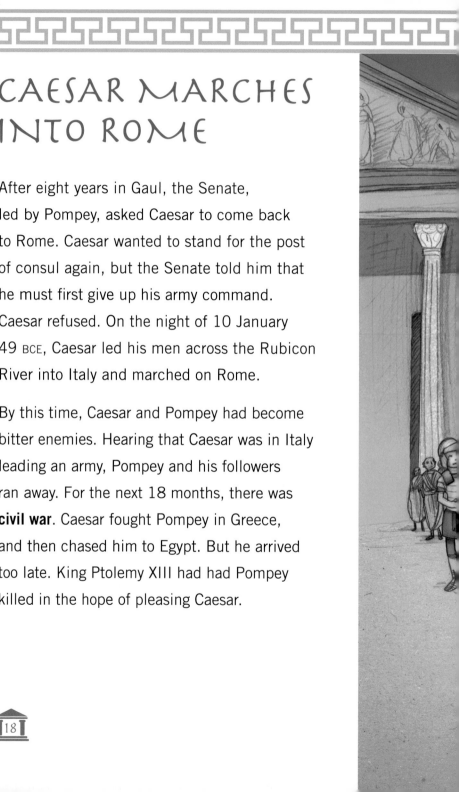

After eight years in Gaul, the Senate, led by Pompey, asked Caesar to come back to Rome. Caesar wanted to stand for the post of consul again, but the Senate told him that he must first give up his army command. Caesar refused. On the night of 10 January 49 BCE, Caesar led his men across the Rubicon River into Italy and marched on Rome.

By this time, Caesar and Pompey had become bitter enemies. Hearing that Caesar was in Italy leading an army, Pompey and his followers ran away. For the next 18 months, there was **civil war**. Caesar fought Pompey in Greece, and then chased him to Egypt. But he arrived too late. King Ptolemy XIII had had Pompey killed in the hope of pleasing Caesar.

EGYPT

While Caesar was in Egypt, he became caught up in a war between King Ptolemy and his sister, Cleopatra. Both wanted to be ruler of Egypt. Caesar took Cleopatra's side, and Ptolemy plotted to kill him.

Battle rages in the Egyptian city of Alexandria.

During one battle, Ptolemy trapped Caesar in the city of Alexandria. The Romans fought back with spears and stormed Ptolemy's camp. As Ptolemy tried to flee, his ship capsized and he was drowned.

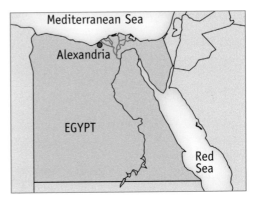

After more than a year of fighting, Caesar had beaten Ptolemy's army, and Cleopatra became queen. By helping Cleopatra, Caesar made sure that the ruler of Egypt was friendly to Rome. This was important because Egypt was a very rich country and could be useful to Rome.

From Egypt, Caesar sailed for Turkey to crush another **uprising** against Roman rule. Caesar and his army beat King Pharnaces in a battle that only lasted for four hours. At the victory celebrations, the soldiers carried banners with the **slogan** "Veni, Vidi, Vici" – "I came, I saw, I conquered".

DICTATOR

After his success in Egypt and Turkey, Caesar returned home to a hero's welcome. The Senate made him dictator. To celebrate, there were spectacular games such as wild-beast hunts, with hundreds of lions, and gladiator fights. There was even a sea battle, with real warships, on a specially flooded lake.

FACT

Caesar also changed the calendar. He set the length of the year at 365 days, based on the time it takes for the Earth to move around the Sun. The year was divided into 12 months. After his death, the month Quintilis was renamed Julius (July) in his honour.

Then Caesar set about changing the way that Rome was run. He wanted to bring the Roman lands together under a strong government. He also passed laws to help poor people and to get rid of **debts**. He built temples, markets and a new Senate House to make Rome look grander.

MURDER!

Caesar was now the most important man in the Roman world. His statues were put up in temples, and his face was stamped on coins.

But not everyone was happy. Some people in Rome thought that Caesar was becoming too powerful. They began to plot secretly against him. The plotters were led by two senators, Cassius and Brutus.

On 15 March 44 BCE, Caesar went to a meeting with other senators. As he arrived, the plotters attacked. Within minutes, Caesar lay dead on the steps of the Senate House, with 23 stab wounds in his body.

The people of Rome were horrified. Thousands of them came to Caesar's funeral, throwing weapons, jewellery and clothes on to the **funeral pyre**. Afterwards, they angrily attacked the houses of Cassius and Brutus.

THE ROMAN EMPIRE

In his will, Caesar named his great-nephew, Octavian, as his son and heir. Octavian wanted revenge for Caesar's death. After many years of civil war, he won control of Rome. He was given a new name, Augustus (which means "honoured one") and became the first **emperor** of Rome. Under Augustus, the lands ruled by the Romans became known as the Roman Empire.

Julius Caesar was a great general who helped Rome to become a huge and powerful force. He was also a brilliant speaker and writer. Many people admired him. But he also wanted riches and power. His life and actions have **inspired** many political leaders, soldiers and writers.

FACT

A famous play about Caesar was written by William Shakespeare in 1599. It tells the story of Caesar's assassination, and has been performed many times around the world.

a statue of Emperor Augustus Caesar in Rome from the 1st century CE

GLOSSARY

arena	an area where shows or events are held
charm	a small object worn as a decoration
civil war	a war between different groups within the same country
conquering	defeating
debts	money or things owed to other people
dictator	a ruler who is in complete control
emperor	another name for a king
funeral pyre	a pile of material, like wood, for burning a body at a ceremony for a person who has died
governed	organised and controlled
governor	a person who's in charge
inspired	encouraged someone to do something
Latin	the language of ancient Rome
pact	agreement
ransom	money demanded in return for setting free a prisoner
slogan	a few words or a short sentence used to convey a message
tactics	ways of getting what you want
toga	a long, loose garment worn in ancient Rome
tunic	a loose, knee-length garment worn in ancient Rome
uprising	an organised movement against the people in charge

INDEX

"I CAME, I SAW, I CONQUERED"

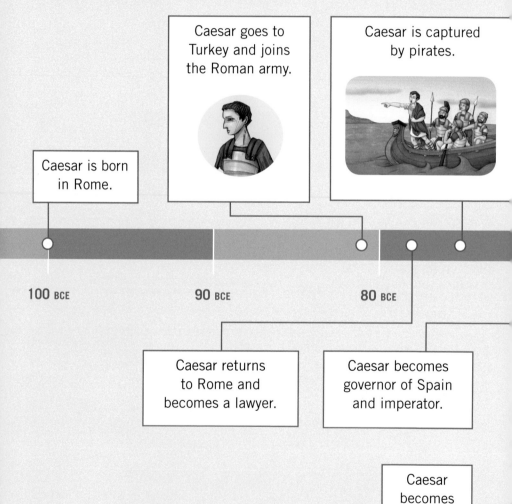

Caesar goes to Turkey and joins the Roman army.

Caesar is captured by pirates.

Caesar is born in Rome.

100 BCE   90 BCE   80 BCE

Caesar returns to Rome and becomes a lawyer.

Caesar becomes governor of Spain and imperator.

Caesar becomes governor of Gaul.

Caesar becomes consul in Rome.

Caesar supports Cleopatra in Egypt.

Caesar becomes dictator of Rome.

Caesar is in charge of entertainment in Rome.

Caesar defeats the Gauls, led by Vercingetorix.

Caesar attacks Britain.

Caesar is murdered by Cassius and Brutus.

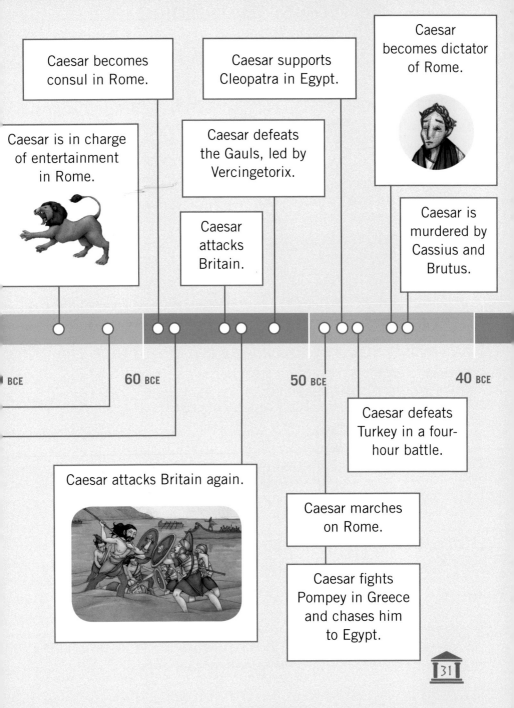

BCE

60 BCE

50 BCE

40 BCE

Caesar defeats Turkey in a four-hour battle.

Caesar attacks Britain again.

Caesar marches on Rome.

Caesar fights Pompey in Greece and chases him to Egypt.

✿ Ideas for reading ✿

Written by Clare Dowdall, PhD
Lecturer and Primary Literacy Consultant

English learning objectives:

- ask questions to improve understanding
- draw inferences such as inferring character's feelings, thoughts and motives from their actions, and justifying inferences with evidence
- retrieve and record information from non-fiction

Spoken language objectives:

- participate in discussions, presentations, performances, roleplay, improvisations and debates

Curriculum links: History – Roman Empire; Geography – locational knowledge; Mathematics – measurement

Resources: globe, atlas or ICT world map, whiteboards, ICT for research, clay and clay tools or paper plates, calendars

Build a context for reading

- Look at the front cover and blurb and help children to read the name *Julius Caesar*. Discuss what they already know about him and the Roman empire.

- Ask children what a "ferocious tyrant" is, and to suggest how Julius Caesar might have behaved to be given this label.

- Find the city of Rome on a map or globe, and note where it is.

Understand and apply reading strategies

- Read the contents together. Ask children how this information book is organised and help them to notice that it is arranged in time order.

- Turn to pp2–3. Read the text aloud and use questioning to help them make connections with their own experience, e.g. *What do we call people who are like senators today?* (politicians).